POEMS

MW01109917

BY
Robert Louis Stevenson, Sara Teasdale, Renee Erickson, Aesop, others

A Genesis Curriculum
Rainbow Reader

Yellow Series
Volume 1

What are the Rainbow Readers?

The Rainbow Readers offer the high-quality literature from the Easy Peasy All-in-One Homeschool in a new format.

When I created the Genesis Curriculum, a year-long science, history and language arts curriculum based on a book of the Bible, I needed a reading option. I wanted to use the literature I had already chosen for Easy Peasy (EP) but didn't need the whole course that came with it. I wanted to allow for a family reading time, where everyone could do their reading for a set amount of time, but I also wanted to enable students to switch into EP at any time life made that preferable.

That's how the idea for the Rainbow Readers was born. These books are the novels and poetry and short stories used in the Easy Peasy levels. Their cover colors go in the order of the rainbow and match the EP Reader levels. Red books are the level one books. Orange books are the level two books, etc. Each color series has numbered volumes to put them in order for you.

What makes the Rainbow Readers different from the EP Readers? Instead of all of the readings being contained in one big book, these are done as individual books. Instead of being split into 180 lessons, they are only split by chapter. Instead of having vocabulary exercises, students are given a dictionary and the words included in it are underlined in the text. Instead of directions, students are to narrate a summary of what they read.

What makes these read-on-your-own books different than ones you'll find elsewhere?
- modern American spelling (eg. colour -> color)
- the included dictionary and underlined vocabulary
- some light editing for content (only a few books)
- occasional helps with explanations or pictures
- scanning errors removed
- reading tips

Reading Tips

Stories should make sense. If you read something that doesn't make any sense, stop and try to figure out what word would make sense there.

Sound out words you are unsure of. When you figure it out, read the sentence again with the word in it.

When you come to an underlined word that you don't know, stop and look it up in the dictionary in the front of this book. Then read the sentence again with your new understanding.

Picture the story in your mind as you read. Watch the action unfold in your imagination. Hear the characters speak. Let the book become a movie in your mind.

Don't get to the end of a chapter and not know what happened. If you ever get lost, go back to where you know what was happening and try again. If you are still lost, ask for help.

You don't have to know every word to understand what's going on. Take clues from what's happening and how the characters are responding. Are they happy? Angry?

When you get to the end of the chapter, tell someone about what happened. Who was the chapter about? What did he do? What did that cause to happen? How does everyone feel about that? Predict what you think is going to happen in the story.

Dictionary

array: to be dressed in a particular way

barren: empty because it doesn't produce (usually describes land where nothing is growing)

beguile: help pass the time, or to charm someone to trick them

billows: large waves or something being puffed up with air

coax: to gently try to convince someone to do something

contemptuous: acting like someone else is beneath you

crest: peak, top of

deceive: to lie, trick

diminish: to lessen

distraught: dismayed, upset

entreat: plead, beg

exquisite: very beautiful

eminent: well-known and respected

fault: a mistake or being responsible for a mistake

gape: opened wide (to gape at someone is to stare at them with your mouth hanging open)

hoax: a bad trick

hue: color

keen: particular, or showing eagerness

obliterate: completely destroy

piteous: used to describe something that you feel sorry for

preposterous: outlandish, unbelievable

provocation: deliberately making someone angry

sage: older, wise man

slumber: sleep

swarm: a large group all clumped together or all moving
      together

swift: fast

tame: opposite of wild

timid: fearful, not brave

tender: gentle and kind

utility: useful

wiles: the tricks used to persuade someone to do what you
      want

Here are some other words that might help.

When it talks about a **nurse**, it's not talking about a hospital. It means a nanny, or a person whose job it is to take care of the children.

These are types of birds: **thrush, swallow**.

These are types of plants: **sorrel, nettle**.

Don't get confused by metaphors in the poems. Metaphors are when they call one thing something else. It helps to describe what's going on. Below is part of the first poem you'll read. It's about building with blocks. I don't know what a kirk is, but I can picture him building a city with blocks. There's not really a harbor and boats, just his living room and his blocks.

> Let the sofa be mountains, the carpet be sea,
> There I'll establish a city for me:
> A kirk and a mill and a palace beside,
> And a harbor as well where my vessels may ride.

Stone Soup

There's a famous story called *Stone Soup*. It's an old French tale about three tired and hungry soldiers who had traveled far before coming into a village to find a place to sleep and to have their stomachs filled.

The villagers saw them coming, but instead of preparing a meal, they hid all of their food. It had been a poor harvest, and they wanted to keep all they had for themselves. They covered the stores of food, hiding everything they could.

When the soldiers came, they asked for a place to spend the night. The villagers insisted that all of their beds were full and there certainly was no room for the strangers.

The soldiers asked for a meal, but every last villager insisted there was no food to spare. Each made an excuse and none offered hospitality.

The soldiers looked at each other. Then one said, "Well then, we'll have to make stone soup."

The villagers were surprised at this. They had made many different kinds of soups but never one from stones. Could it be possible? There were many stones around. What if they each could be made into soup?

The soldier chose three smooth stones for the soup and asked for a large iron pot to cook it in. The villagers were so curious at how to make stone soup that someone offered a pot.

The stones were placed inside it, water was poured into it, and a fire was lit under it. The soldiers looked satisfied, but said, "Any soup needs salt and pepper." The villagers agreed and one ran to get them. The soldiers added them to the pot and the villagers were wondering what kind of soup was coming to a boil.

1

The soldiers began to talk amongst themselves. "Stone soup is wonderful, but carrots make it even better." The villagers looked at one another and one ran to get carrots out from under a blanket.

The soldiers then began to say how if there were potatoes and a bit of beef it would be good enough for any rich man's table. The sound of that was tempting to the poor villagers, and two ran off to provide potatoes and beef for the stone soup.

One more time the soldiers spoke among themselves about the soup. "When the king dined with us, he loved this very soup with just a bit of barley and milk." This was a king's meal, all from stones! The villagers were so excited that they had the soup of kings in their village that they brought to the pot barley and milk.

The soldiers announced that the soup would soon be ready and that the soldiers would give a taste to them all. Now the villagers began to talk among themselves and say that such a soup should have bread and a roast and cider. It wasn't long before the tables were set and a feast was spread before them all.

Everyone was sure it was the best soup they had ever tasted. And to think, it was made from stones!

Poems by Robert Louis Stevenson

BLOCK CITY

What are you able to build with your blocks?
Castles and palaces, temples and docks.
Rain may keep raining and others go roam,
But I can be happy and building at home.

Let the sofa be mountains, the carpet be sea,
There I'll establish a city for me:
A kirk and a mill and a palace beside,
And a harbor as well where my vessels may
ride.

Great is the palace with pillar and wall,
A sort of a tower on the top of it all,
And steps coming down in an orderly way
To where my toy vessels lay safe in the bay.

This one is sailing and that one is moored:
Hark to the song of the sailors on board!
And see the steps of my palace, the kings
Coming and going with presents and things!

Now I have done with it, down let it go!
All in a moment the town is laid low.
Block upon block lying scattered and free,
What is there left of my town by the sea?

Yet as I saw it, I see it again,
The kirk and the palace, the ships and the men
And as long as I live and where'er I may be,
I'll always remember my town by the sea.

BED IN SUMMER

In winter I get up at night,
And dress by yellow candle light.
In summer quite the other way,
I have to go to bed by day.
I have to go to bed and see

The birds still hopping on the tree,
Or hear the grown-up people's feet,
Still going past me in the street.
And does it not seem hard to you,
When all the sky is clear and blue,
And I should like so much to play,
To have to go to bed by day?

YOUNG NIGHT THOUGHT

All night long and every night,
When my mamma puts out the light
I see the people marching by,
As plain as day, before my eye.

Armies and emperors and kings,
All carrying different kinds of things,
And marching in so grand a way,
You never saw the like by day.

So fine a show was never seen
At the great circus on the green;
For every kind beast and man
Is marching in that caravan.

At first they move a little slow,
But still the faster on they go,
And still beside them close I keep
Until we reach the Town of Sleep.

4

A GOOD PLAY

We built a ship upon the stairs
All made of the back-bedroom chairs,
And filled it full of sofa pillows
To go a-sailing on the billows.

We took a saw and several nails,
And water in the nursery pails;
And Tom said, "Let us also take
An apple and a slice of cake;"

—Which was enough for Tom and me
To go a-sailing on, till tea.
We sailed along for days and days,
And had the very best of plays;
But Tom fell out and hurt his knee,
So there was no one left but me.

THE MOON

The moon has a face like the clock in the hall;
She shines on thieves on the garden wall,
On streets and fields and harbor quays,
And birdies asleep in the forks of the trees.

The squalling cat and the squeaking mouse,
The howling dog by the door of the house,
The bat that lies in bed at noon,
All love to be out by the light of the moon.

But all of the things that belong to the day
Cuddle to sleep to be out of her way;
And flowers and children close their eyes
Till up in the morning the sun shall rise.

5

THE COW

The friendly cow all red and white,
I love with all my heart:
She gives me cream with all her might,
To eat with apple-tart.
She wanders lowing here and there,
And yet she cannot stray,
All in the pleasant open air,
The pleasant light of day.
And blown by all the winds that pass
And wet with all the showers,
She walks among the meadow grass
And eats the meadow flowers.

AT THE SEASIDE

When I was down beside the sea,
A wooden spade they gave to me
To dig the sandy shore.
My holes were hollow like a cup,
In every hole the sea came up,
Till it could hold no more.

HAPPY THOUGHT

The world is so full of a number of things,
I'm sure we should all be as happy as kings.

THE LAND OF NOD

From breakfast on through all the day
At home among my friends I stay,
But every night I go abroad
Afar into the Land of Nod.

All by myself I have to go,
With none to tell me what to do—
All alone beside the streams
And up the mountain-sides of dreams.

The strangest things are there for me,
Both things to eat and things to see,
And many frightening sights abroad
Till morning in the Land of Nod.

Try as I like to find the way,
I never can get back by day,
Nor can remember plain and clear
The curious music that I hear.

MY SHADOW

I have a little shadow that goes in and out with me,
And what can be the use of him is more than I can see.
He is very, very like me, from the heels up to the head;
And I see him jump before me, when I jump into my bed.

The funniest thing about him is the way he likes to grow—
Not at all like proper children, which is always very slow;
For he sometimes shoots up taller, like an india-rubber ball,
And he sometimes gets so little that there's none of him at all.

He hasn't got a notion of how children ought to play,
And can only make a fool of me in every sort of way.

He stays so close beside me, he's a coward you can see;
I'd think shame to stick to nursie as that shadow sticks to me!

One morning, very early, before the sun was up,
I 'rose and found the shining dew on every buttercup;
But my lazy little shadow, like an arrant sleepy head,
Had stayed at home behind me and was fast asleep in bed.

SINGING

Of speckled eggs the birdie sings
And nests among the trees;
The sailor sings of ropes and things
In ships upon the seas.
The children sing in far Japan,
The children sing in Spain;
The organ with the organ man
Is singing in the rain.

MY BED IS A BOAT

My bed is like a little boat;
Nurse helps me in when I embark;
She girds me in my sailor's coat
And starts me in the dark.

At night, I go on board and say
Good night to all my friends on shore;
I shut my eyes and sail away
And see and hear no more.

And sometimes things to bed I take,
As prudent sailors have to do;
Perhaps a slice of wedding-cake,
Perhaps a toy or two.

All night across the dark we steer:
But when the day returns at last
Safe in my room, beside the pier,
I find my vessel fast.

RAIN

The rain is raining all around.
It falls on field and tree,
It rains on the umbrellas here,
And on the ships at sea.

THE WIND

I saw you toss the kites on high
And blow the birds about the sky;
And all around I heard you pass,
Like ladies' skirts across the grass—

O wind, a-blowing all day long!
O wind, that sings so loud a song!
I saw the different things you did,
But always you yourself you hid.

I felt you push, I heard you call,
I could not see yourself at all—
O wind, a-blowing all day long,
O wind, that sings so loud a song!

O you that are so strong and cold,
O blower, are you young or old?
Are you a beast of field and tree,
Or just a stronger child than me?
O wind, a-blowing all day long,
O wind, that sings so loud a song!

A GOOD BOY

I woke before the morning, I was happy all the day,
I never said an ugly word, but smiled and stuck to play.
And now at last the sun is going down behind the wood,
And I am very happy, for I know that I've been good.
My bed is waiting cool and fresh, with linen smooth and fair,
And I must off to sleepsin-by, and not forget my prayer.
I know that, till tomorrow I shall see the sun arise,
No ugly dream shall fright my mind, no ugly sight my eyes.
But slumber hold me tightly, till I waken in the dawn,
And hear the thrushes singing in the lilacs round the lawn.

THE SWING

How do you like to go up in a swing,
Up in the air so blue?
Oh, I do think it the pleasantest thing
Ever a child can do!

Up in the air and over the wall,
Till I can see so wide,
Rivers and trees and cattle and all
Over the countryside—
Till I look down on the garden green,
Down on the roof so brown—
Up in the air I go flying again,
Up in the air and down!

THE LITTLE LAND

When at home alone I sit
And am very tired of it,
I have just to shut my eyes
To go sailing through the skies—

To go sailing far away
To the pleasant Land of play;
To the fairy land afar
Where the Little People are;

Where the clover-tops are trees,
And the rain-pools are the seas,
And the leaves like little ships
Sail about on tiny trips;

And above the daisy tree
Through the grasses,
High o'erhead the Bumble Bee
Hums and passes.

In that forest to and fro
I can wander, I can go;
See the spider and the fly,
And the ants go marching by

Carrying parcels with their feet
Down the green and grassy street.
I can in the sorrel sit
Where the ladybird alit.

I can climb the jointed grass;
And on high
See the greater swallows pass
In the sky,

And the round sun rolling by
Heeding no such things as I.
Through that forest I can pass
Till, as in a looking-glass,

Humming fly and daisy tree
And my tiny self I see,
Painted very clear and neat
On the rain-pool at my feet.

Should a leaflet come to land
Drifting near to where I stand,
Straight I'll board that tiny boat
Round the rain-pool sea to float.

Little thoughtful creatures sit
On the grassy coasts of it;
Little things with lovely eyes
See me sailing with surprise.

Some are clad in armor green—
(These have sure to battle been!)—
Some are pied with ev'ry <u>hue</u>,
Black and crimson, gold and blue;

Some have wings and <u>swift</u> are gone;
But they all look kindly on.
When my eyes I once again
Open, and see all things plain;

High bare walls, great bare floor;
Great big knobs on drawer and door;
Great big people perched on chairs,
Stitching tucks and mending tears,

Each a hill that I could climb,
And talking nonsense all the time—
O dear me,
That I could be

A sailor on the rain-pool sea,
A climber in, the clover tree,
And just come back, a sleepy-head,
Late at night to go to bed.

Poems by William Blake

Piping down the valleys wild,
Piping songs of pleasant glee,
On a cloud I saw a child,
And he laughing said to me:

'Pipe a song about a Lamb!'
So I piped with merry cheer.
'Piper, pipe that song again.'
So I piped: he wept to hear.

'Drop thy pipe, thy happy pipe;
Sing thy songs of happy cheer!'
So I sung the same again,
While he wept with joy to hear.

'Piper, sit thee down and write
In a book, that all may read.'
So he vanished from my sight;
And I plucked a hollow reed,

And I made a rural pen,
And I stained the water clear,
And I wrote my happy songs
Every child may joy to hear.

THE SHEPHERD

How sweet is the shepherd's sweet lot!
From the morn to the evening he strays;
He shall follow his sheep all the day,
And his tongue shall be filled with praise.

For he hears the lambs' innocent call,
And he hears the ewes' <u>tender</u> reply;
He is watchful while they are in peace,
For they know when their shepherd is nigh.

THE ECHOING GREEN

The sun does arise,
And make happy the skies;
The merry bells ring
To welcome the Spring;
The skylark and thrush,
The birds of the bush,
Sing louder around
To the bells' cheerful sound;
While our sports shall be seen
On the echoing green.

Old John, with white hair,
Does laugh away care,
Sitting under the oak,
Among the old folk.
They laugh at our play,
And soon they all say,
'Such, such were the joys
When we all -- girls and boys --
In our youth-time were seen
On the echoing green.'

Till the little ones, weary,
No more can be merry:
The sun does descend,
And our sports have an end.
Round the laps of their mothers
Many sisters and brothers,
Like birds in their nest,
Are ready for rest,
And sport no more seen
On the darkening green.

THE LAMB

Little lamb, who made thee?
Dost thou know who made thee,
Gave thee life, and bid thee feed
By the stream and o'er the mead;
Gave thee clothing of delight,
Softest clothing, woolly, bright;
Gave thee such a <u>tender</u> voice,
Making all the vales rejoice?
Little lamb, who made thee?
Dost thou know who made thee?

Little lamb, I'll tell thee;
Little lamb, I'll tell thee:
He is called by thy name,
For He calls Himself a Lamb.
He is meek, and He is mild,
He became a little child.
I a child, and thou a lamb,
We are called by His name.
Little lamb, God bless thee!
Little lamb, God bless thee!

LAUGHING SONG

When the green woods laugh with the voice of joy,
And the dimpling stream runs laughing by;
When the air does laugh with our merry wit,
And the green hill laughs with the noise of it;

When the meadows laugh with lively green,
And the grasshopper laughs in the merry scene;
When Mary and Susan and Emily
With their sweet round mouths sing 'Ha ha he!'

When the painted birds laugh in the shade,
Where our table with cherries and nuts is spread:
Come live, and be merry, and join with me,
To sing the sweet chorus of 'Ha ha he!'

A CRADLE SONG

Sweet dreams, form a shade
O'er my lovely infant's head!
Sweet dreams of pleasant streams
By happy, silent, moony beams!

Sweet Sleep, with soft down
Weave thy brows an infant crown!
Sweet Sleep, angel mild,
Hover o'er my happy child!

Sweet smiles, in the night
Hover over my delight!
Sweet smiles, mother's smiles,
All the livelong night beguiles.

Sweet moans, dovelike sighs,
Chase not slumber from thy eyes!
Sweet moans, sweeter smiles,
All the dovelike moans beguiles.

Sleep, sleep, happy child!
All creation slept and smiled.
Sleep, sleep, happy sleep,
While o'er thee thy mother weep.

Sweet babe, in thy face
Holy image I can trace;
Sweet babe, once like thee
Thy Maker lay, and wept for me:

Wept for me, for thee, for all,
When He was an infant small.
Thou His image ever see,
Heavenly face that smiles on thee!

Smiles on thee, on me, on all,
Who became an infant small;
Infant smiles are His own smiles;
Heaven and earth to peace beguiles.

SPRING

Sound the flute!
Now it's mute!
Birds delight,
Day and night,
Nightingale,
In the dale,
Lark in sky, --
Merrily,
Merrily, merrily to welcome in the year.

Little boy,
Full of joy;
Little girl,
Sweet and small;
Cock does crow,

17

So do you;
Merry voice,
Infant noise;
Merrily, merrily to welcome in the year.

Little lamb,
Here I am;
Come and lick
My white neck;
Let me pull
Your soft wool;
Let me kiss
Your soft face;
Merrily, merrily we welcome in the year.

NURSE'S SONG

When voices of children are heard on the green,
And laughing is heard on the hill,
My heart is at rest within my breast,
And everything else is still.
'Then come home, my children, the sun is gone down,
And the dews of night arise;
Come, come, leave off play, and let us away,
Till the morning appears in the skies.'

'No, no, let us play, for it is yet day,
And we cannot go to sleep;
Besides, in the sky the little birds fly,
And the hills are all covered with sheep.'
'Well, well, go and play till the light fades away,
And then go home to bed.'
The little ones leaped, and shouted, and laughed,
And all the hills echoed.

INFANT JOY

'I have no name;
I am but two days old.'
What shall I call thee?
'I happy am,
Joy is my name.'
Sweet joy befall thee!

Pretty joy!
Sweet joy, but two days old.
Sweet joy I call thee:
Thou dost smile,
I sing the while;
Sweet joy befall thee!

THE FLY

Little Fly,
Thy summer's play
My thoughtless hand
Has brushed away.

Am not I
A fly like thee?
Or art not thou
A man like me?

For I dance,
And drink, and sing,
Till some blind hand
Shall brush my wing.

If thought is life
And strength and breath,
And the want
Of thought is death;

Then am I
A happy fly.
If I live,
Or if I die.

A CRADLE SONG

Sleep, sleep, beauty bright,
Dreaming in the joys of night;
Sleep, sleep; in thy sleep
Little sorrows sit and weep.
Sweet babe, in thy face
Soft desires I can trace,
Secret joys and secret smiles,
Little pretty infant wiles.
As thy softest limbs I feel,
Smiles as of the morning steal
O'er thy cheek, and o'er thy breast
Where thy little heart doth rest.
O the cunning wiles that creep
In thy little heart asleep!
When thy little heart doth wake,
Then the dreadful light shall break.
From thy cheek and from thy eye
O'er the youthful harvest nigh
Infant wiles and infant smiles
Heaven and Earth of peace beguiles.

Poems by Sara Teasdale

WISHES

I wish for such a lot of things
That never will come true--
And yet I want them all so much
I think they might, don't you?

I want a little kitty-cat
That's soft and <u>tame</u> and sweet,
And every day I watch and hope
I'll find one in the street.

But nursie says, "Come, walk along,
"Don't stand and stare like that"--
I'm only looking hard and hard
To try to find my cat.

And then I want a blue balloon
That tries to fly away,
I thought if I wished hard enough
That it would come someday.

One time when I was in the park
I knew that it would be
Beside the big old clock at home
A-waiting there for me--

And soon as we got home again,
I hurried thro' the hall,
And looked beside the big old clock--
It wasn't there at all.

I think I'll never wish again--
But then, what shall I do?
The wishes are a lot of fun
Altho' they don't come true.

FAULTS

They came to tell your <u>fault</u>s to me,
They named them over one by one,
I laughed aloud when they were done;
I knew them all so well before,--
Oh they were blind, too blind to see
Your <u>fault</u>s had made me love you more.

SNOW SONG

Fairy snow, fairy snow,
Blowing, blowing everywhere,
Would that I
Too, could fly
Lightly, lightly through the air.

NOVEMBER

The world is tired, the year is old,
The little leaves are glad to die,
The wind goes shivering with cold
Among the rushes dry.

DAWN

The greenish sky glows up in misty reds,
The purple shadows turn to brick and stone,
The dreams wear thin, men turn upon their beds,
And hear the milk-cart jangle by alone.

22

GRANDFATHER'S LOVE

They said he sent his love to me,
They wouldn't put it in my hand,
And when I asked them where it was
They said I couldn't understand.

I thought they must have hidden it,
I hunted for it all the day,
And when I told them so at night
They smiled and turned their heads away.

They say that love is something kind,
That I can never see or touch.
I wish he'd sent me something else,
I like his cough-drops twice as much.

THE KIND MOON

I think the moon is very kind
To take such trouble just for me.
He came along with me from home
To keep me company.

He went as fast as I could run;
I wonder how he crossed the sky?
I'm sure he hasn't legs and feet
Or any wings to fly.

Yet here he is above their roof;
Perhaps he thinks it isn't right
For me to go so far alone,
Tho' mother said I might.

APRIL

The roofs are shining from the rain,
The sparrows twitter as they fly,
And with a windy April grace
The little clouds go by.
Yet the back yards are bare and brown
With only one unchanging tree-
I could not be so sure of Spring
Save that it sings in me.

DUSK IN JUNE

Evening, and all the birds
In a chorus of shimmering sound
Are easing their hearts of joy
For miles around.

The air is blue and sweet,
The few first stars are white,
Oh let me like the birds
Sing before night.

THE CLOUD

I am a cloud in the heaven's height,
The stars are lit for my delight,
Tireless and changeful, swift and free,
I cast my shadow on hill and sea
But why do the pines on the mountain's crest
Call to me always, "Rest, rest"?

I throw my mantle over the moon
And I blind the sun on his throne at noon,
Nothing can tame me, nothing can bind,
I am a child of the heartless wind

24

But oh the pines on the mountain's <u>crest</u>
Whispering always, "Rest, rest."

IN THE CARPENTER'S SHOP

Mary sat in the corner dreaming,
Dim was the room and low,
While in the dusk, the saw went screaming
To and fro.

Jesus and Joseph toiled together,
Mary was watching them,
Thinking of kings in the wintry weather
At Bethlehem.

Mary sat in the corner thinking,
Jesus had grown a man;
One by one her hopes were sinking
As the years ran.

Jesus and Joseph toiled together,
Mary's thoughts were far
Angels sang in the wintry weather
Under a star.

Mary sat in the corner weeping,
Bitter and hot her tears
Little faith were the angels keeping
All the years.

Poems by various authors

THE ARROW AND THE SONG
by Longfellow

I shot an arrow into the air,
It fell to earth, I knew not where;
For, so <u>swift</u>ly it flew, the sight
Could not follow it in its flight.
I breathed a song into the air,
It fell to earth, I knew not where;

For who has sight so <u>keen</u> and strong
That it can follow the flight of song?
Long, long afterward, in an oak
I found the arrow, still unbroke;
And the song, from beginning to end,
I found again in the heart of a friend.

LET DOGS DELIGHT TO BARK AND BITE
by Isaac Watts

Let dogs delight to bark and bite,
For God hath made them so;
Let bears and lions growl and fight,
For 'tis their nature too.
But, children, you should never let
Such angry passions rise;
Your little hands were never made
To tear each other's eyes.

LITTLE THINGS
by Ebenezer Brewer

Little drops of water,
Little grains of sand,
Make the mighty ocean
And the pleasant land.
Thus the little minutes,
Humble though they be,
Make the mighty ages
Of eternity.

SWEET AND LOW
by Alfred Tennyson

Sweet and low, sweet and low,
Wind of the western sea,
Low, low, breathe and blow,
Wind of the western sea!
Over the rolling waters go,
Come from the dropping moon and blow,
Blow him again to me;
While my little one, while my pretty one sleeps.
Sleep and rest, sleep and rest,
Father will come to thee soon;
Rest, rest, on mother's breast,
Father will come to thee soon;
Father will come to his babe in the nest,
Silver sails all out of the west
Under the silver moon:
Sleep, my little one, sleep, my pretty one, sleep.

LILY WHITE
by George MacDonald.

Rebecca Giles

Little White Lily
Sat by a stone,
Drooping and waiting
Till the sun shone.

Little White Lily
Sunshine has fed;
Little White Lily
Is lifting her head.

Little White Lily
Said: "It is good
Little White Lily's
Clothing and food."

Little White Lily
Dressed like a bride!
Shining with whiteness,
And crowned beside!

Little White Lily
Drooping with pain,
Waiting and waiting
For the wet rain.

Little White Lily
Holdeth her cup;
Rain is fast falling
And filling it up.

Little White Lily
Said: "Good again,
When I am thirsty
To have the nice rain.

Now I am stronger,
Now I am cool;
Heat cannot burn me,
My veins are so full."

Little White Lily
Smells very sweet;
On her head sunshine,
Rain at her feet.

Thanks to the sunshine,
Thanks to the rain,
Little White Lily
Is happy again.

HOW THE LEAVES CAME DOWN
by Susan Coolidge

"I'll tell you how the leaves came down,"
The great Tree to his children said:
"You're getting sleepy, Yellow and Brown,
Yes, very sleepy, little Red.
It is quite time to go to bed."

"Ah!" begged each silly, pouting leaf,
"Let us a little longer stay;
Dear Father Tree, behold our grief!
Tis such a very pleasant day,
We do not want to go away."

So, for just one more merry day
To the great Tree the leaflets clung,
Frolicked and danced, and had their way,
Upon the autumn breezes swung,
Whispering all their sports among—

"Perhaps the great Tree will forget,
And let us stay until the spring,
If we all beg, and coax, and fret.
"But the great Tree did no such thing;
He smiled to hear their whispering.

"Come, children, all to bed," he cried;
And ere the leaves could urge their prayer,
He shook his head, and far and wide,
Fluttering and rustling everywhere,
Down sped the leaflets through the air.

I saw them; on the ground they lay,
Golden and red, a huddled swarm,
Waiting till one from far away,
White bedclothes heaped upon her arm,
Should come to wrap them safe and warm.

30

The great bare Tree looked down and smiled.
"Good-night, dear little leaves," he said.
And from below each sleepy child
Replied, "Good-night," and murmured,
"It is *so* nice to go to bed!"

WYNKEN, BLYNKEN, AND NOD
by Eugene Field

[Note: You say that winkin' like winking.
It's winkin', blinkin' and nod.]

Wynken, Blynken, and Nod one night
Sailed off in a wooden shoe,—
Sailed on a river of crystal light
Into a sea of dew.

"Where are you going, and what do you wish?
"The old moon asked the three."
We have come to fish for the herring-fish
That live in this beautiful sea;
Nets of silver and gold have we,"
Said Wynken, Blynken, And Nod.

The old moon laughed and sang a song,
As they rocked in the wooden shoe;
And the wind that sped them all night long
Ruffled the waves of dew;

The little stars were the herring-fish
That lived in the beautiful sea.
"Now cast your nets wherever you wish,—
Never afeard are we!"
So cried the stars to the fishermen three,
Wynken, Blynken, And Nod.

All night long their nets they threw
To the stars in the twinkling foam,—
Then down from the skies came the wooden shoe,
Bringing the fishermen home:

Twas all so pretty a sail, it seemed
As if it could not be;
And some folk thought 'twas a dream they'd dreamed
Of sailing that beautiful sea;
But I shall name you the fishermen three:
Wynken,Blynken,And Nod.

Wynken and Blynken are two little eyes,
And Nod is a little head,
And the wooden shoe that sailed the skies
Is a wee one's trundle-bed;

So shut your eyes while Mother sings
Of wonderful sights that be,
And you shall see the beautiful things
As you rock on the misty sea
Where the old shoe rocked the fishermen three,
Wynken,Blynken,And Nod.

IF I HAD BUT TWO LITTLE WINGS
by Samuel Taylor Coleridge

If I had but two little wings
And were a little feathery bird,
To you I'd fly, my dear!
But thoughts like these are idle things
And I stay here.
But in my sleep to you I fly:
I'm always with you in my sleep!
The world is all one's own.
And then one wakes, and where am I?
All, all alone.

32

THE VIOLET
by Jane Taylor

Down in a green and shady bed
A modest violet grew;
Its stalk was bent, it hung its head,
As if to hide from view.

And yet it was a lovely flower,
No colors bright and fair;
It might have graced a rosy bower,
Instead of hiding there.

Yet there it was content to bloom,
In modest tints arrayed;
And there diffused its sweet perfume,
Within the silent shade.

Then let me to the valley go,
This pretty flower to see;
That I may also learn to grow
In sweet humility.

A VISIT FROM ST. NICHOLAS
by Clement Clarke Moore

'Twas the night before Christmas, when all through the house
Not a creature was stirring, not even a mouse;

The stockings were hung by the chimney with care,
In hopes that St. Nicholas soon would be there;

The children were nestled all snug in their beds,
While visions of sugar-plums danced in their heads;

And mamma in her 'kerchief, and I in my cap,
Had just settled our brains for a long winter's nap,

33

When out on the lawn there arose such a clatter,
I sprang from the bed to see what was the matter.

Away to the window I flew like a flash,
Tore open the shutters and threw up the sash.

The moon on the breast of the new-fallen snow
Gave the luster of mid-day to objects below,

When, what to my wondering eyes should appear,
But a miniature sleigh, and eight tiny reindeer.

With a little old driver, so lively and quick,
I knew in a moment it must be St. Nick.

More rapid than eagles his coursers they came,
And he whistled, and shouted, and called them by name:

"Now, *Dasher*! now, *Dancer*! now, *Prancer* and *Vixen*!
On, *Comet*! on, *Cupid*! on, *Donder* and *Blitzen*!

To the top of the porch! to the top of the wall!
Now dash away! dash away! dash away all!"

As dry leaves that before the wild hurricane fly,
When they meet with an obstacle, mount to the sky;

So up to the house-top the coursers they flew,
With the sleigh full of toys, and St. Nicholas, too.

And then, in a twinkling, I heard on the roof
The prancing and pawing of each little hoof.

As I drew in my head, and was turning around,
Down the chimney St. Nicholas came with a bound.

He was dressed all in fur, from his head to his foot,
And his clothes were all tarnished with ashes and soot;

A bundle of toys he had flung on his back,
And he looked like a peddler just opening his pack.

His eyes—how they twinkled! his dimples how merry!
His cheeks were like roses, his nose like a cherry!

His droll little mouth was drawn up like a bow,
And the beard of his chin was as white as the snow;

The stump of a pipe he held tight in his teeth,
And the smoke it encircled his head like a wreath;

He had a broad face and a little round belly,
That shook when he laughed, like a bowlful of jelly.

He was chubby and plump, a right jolly old elf,
And I laughed when I saw him, in spite of myself;

A wink of his eye and a twist of his head,
Soon gave me to know I had nothing to dread;

He spoke not a word, but went straight to his work,
And filled all the stockings; then turned with a jerk,

And laying his finger aside of his nose,
And giving a nod, up the chimney he rose;

He sprang to his sleigh, to his team gave a whistle,
And away they all flew like the down on a thistle.

But I heard him exclaim, ere he drove out of sight,"
Happy Christmas to all, and to all a good-night."

FATHER WILLIAM
by Lewis Carroll

"You are old, Father William," the young man said,
"And your hair has become very white;
And yet you incessantly stand on your head—
Do you think, at your age, it is right?"

"In my youth," Father William replied to his son,
"I feared it might injure the brain;
But now that I'm perfectly sure I have none,
Why, I do it again and again."

"You are old," said the youth, "as I mentioned before,
And have grown most uncommonly fat;
Yet you turned a back-somersault in at the door—
Pray, what is the reason of that?"

"In my youth," said the <u>sage</u>, as he shook his gray locks,
"I kept all my limbs very supple
By the use of this ointment—one shilling the box—
Allow me to sell you a couple."

"You are old," said the youth, "and your jaws are too weak
For anything tougher than suet;
Yet you finished the goose, with the bones and the beak:
Pray, how did you manage to do it?"

"In my youth," said his father, "I took to the law,
And argued each case with my wife;
And the muscular strength which it gave to my jaw
Has lasted the rest of my life."

"You are old," said the youth; "one would hardly suppose
That your eye was as steady as ever;
Yet you balanced an eel on the end of your nose—
What made you so awfully clever?"

"I have answered three questions, and that is enough,
"Said his father, "don't give yourself airs!
Do you think I can listen all day to such stuff?
Be off, or I'll kick you down-stairs!"

A Play

An Adaptation of the story of five Chinese brothers by Renee Erickson

Cast:
>Emperor
>4 Court Attendants: Han, Chin, Lu, Shou
>2 Court Guards: Sha, Huang
>6 Imperial Guards: Peng, Bo, Wong, Min, Sung, Ming
>5 Children: Deng, Chou, Jiang, Li, Yan
>2 Parents: Zian, Mah
>Narrators / Water bearers (the Sea & the Fleet)

Scene I:

Emperor: behind the screen

4 Court Attendants / 2 Court Guards: stage right "frozen" at chores

6 Imperial Guards: Upstage center, clustered near the benches, "frozen"

5 Children: Stage left, "frozen" in front of the dungeon wall

2 Parents/Narrators: Downstage center – reading from a scroll

Narrator 1: Sometimes it's not easy to know where a piece of the puzzle fits. It can turn out to be quite a surprise, as in our version of an old, old folk tale.

Narrator 2: Once upon a time and long ago in a far, far kingdom by the sea lived a people who knew what was important.

Narrators: (move downstage left)

Guards: (unfreeze but remain in position of disinterest and boredom)

Children: (move downstage and sit on the steps, observing the scene)

Court Persons & Court Guards: (stand as they speak, dramatically emphasizing their attributes – stay standing)

Huang: It's important to be handsome. I'm glad I'm handsome.

Chin: It's important to be smart. I'm glad I'm smart.

Han: It's important to be fast. I'm glad I'm fast.

Emperor: (comes from behind the screen and listens a moment)

Shou: It's important to be strong. I'm glad I'm strong.

Sha: It's important to be tall. I'm glad I'm tall.

Lu: It's important to be graceful. I'm glad I'm graceful.

Emperor: (moves downstage to the throne) It's important to obey the emperor. I'm glad I'm the Emperor. (moves to the throne and sits)

Guards: (snap to attention)

All Court Persons: (bow and kneel to Emperor)

Han, Chin: (exit behind screen)

Lu & Shou: (move downstage to stairs and sit)

Court Guards: (stand beside the throne)

Narrator #1: But, she isn't (motions "tall")

Narrator #2: It doesn't matter. She is the emperor.

Emperor: (moves to the throne) (Clap Clap) Servants of the kitchen!

Han & Chin: (hurry in from the screen – bowing – move to center stage facing the emperor) Yes, emperor. Yes, emperor.

Emperor: My breakfast is late. Why is that?

Han: We're sorry, O imperial one, but the stove could not be lit.

Chin: Yes, o exalted one, someone left the cover off the woodpile last night and all the wood got wet from the rain.

Emperor: And who was that someone?

Han: Not me!

Chin: Not me!

Emperor: Well, who was it?

Han: It was that short, clumsy cook's helper.

Chin: It was all his fault.

Emperor: (considering a moment) Off with his head! (Clap, clap) Guards, see to it!

Peng & Bo: (moving from Up stage center to Center facing Stage right) (bowing to the emperor) Yes, your imperialness.

Peng & Bo: (Bowing, back away from the throne, exit behind the screen)

Offstage (sound of a loud whack.)

Court Guards and all on stage: (shudder)

Emperor: (claps hands) Servants of the bed chamber!

Lu & Shou: (stand up with bowed heads, come to Center stage facing Stage right – the emperor)

Lu: Yes, O most magnificent emperor.

Shou: Yes, o royal one?

Emperor: (with a flourish!) Where is the red robe that I wanted to wear this morning?

Lu: (apologetically and fearfully) Oh, your royalness. It is ruined.

Shou: (apologetically and fearfully) A most unfortunate accident, your majesty.

Emperor: What sort of accident?

Lu: The not very pretty chambermaid mistakenly thought that she could wash it in hot water and (shrugs) all the color came out.

Shou: Alas, it is now a streaky pink and very wrinkled. It was all her <u>fault</u>.

Emperor: (thinks a moment) Off with her head. (clap, clap) Guards, see to it.

Sung & Ming: (moving from Upstage center to center facing Stage right) (bowing to the emperor) (move to exit behind the screen)

Off stage sound of a whack. All shudder.

Han & Chin: (enter bowing, but happy) Please excuse us, Your majesty.

Emperor: What now?

Chin: O, your royalness, we have finally lit the fire. Would you like to come into the breakfast room for your royal breakfast?

Emperor: Indeed. Guards, come with me. (exits behind screen)

Sha & Huang: (move throne to the wall stage right and exit behind the screen with the emperor)

All: exit behind screen

Scene II.

Lights come on to seaside garden wall home of "poor" family.

Children: (come up from the stairs and are seated, mending a fish net, etc.)

Zian and Mah: (stand and move to center stage) They look at their children and consider their attributes and their future.

Narrator 3: (standing down stage center) In the far away kingdom by the sea people also knew who was not important. (pauses then exits behind screen)

Mah: Zian, how could we have been so unfortunate?

Zian: What do you mean, Mah? We have five fine children. We are very fortunate.

Mah: We have five children. I don't know where you got the idea of fine. Are they tall?

Zian: (pauses) No

Mah: Are they handsome?

Zian: (pauses) No

Mah: Are they smart?

Zian: (pauses) Not especially.

Mah: Are they rich?

Zian: (pauses) By no means.

Mah: Are they fast?

Zian: (pauses) Are you kidding?

Mah: Well, are they graceful?

Zian: (annoyed) Well, you should know. But, Mah, they are kind and loving children.

Mah: You are right, Zian, but they just don't have any qualities that anyone thinks are important.

Zian: Mah, have you forgotten that each one has a very special ability?

Mah: (now she's annoyed) Remind me.

Yan: (standing) Don't you remember, mother. Deng can swallow the sea.

Deng: (standing) And Chou has an iron neck.

Chou: (standing) And Jiang can stretch and stretch and stretch.

Jiang: (standing) Li cannot be burned.

Li: (standing) And Yan can hold his breath forever if need be.

Mah: Children, I know you have all these qualities, but what good are they? Have you EVER needed them?

Chou: Not so far, but you never know. They might come in handy sometime.

Mah: I'll tell you what would come in handy - some extra money.

Zian: Your mother speaks the truth, children. Go out and see if you can make yourselves useful. Perhaps you can earn a few coins for your efforts.

Mah: (shrugs and smiles at the children and pats them as they leave) You may not be strong, but you are willing.

Parents: (exit behind the wall)

Children: (sit back to their work, pause, count 15 seconds)

Yan: (standing) I'm not very willing! It's too hot to work.

Deng: (standing) I agree.

Chou: (standing) Let's walk by the sea a bit before we try to be useful.

Children: (walk to center stage and look to upstage left - seaside)

Jiang: (pointing) Li, isn't that the emperor's new fleet of ships?

Li: (shading his eyes) You're right. Don't they look beautiful out there on the horizon?

Yan: Deng, we could get a better look at them if you would swallow the sea and pull them closer to shore.

Li: (getting very excited) Maybe we could even climb aboard and look around.

Deng: I'm not so sure I should. The emperor might not like it.

Jiang: How would he ever know? He's probably up at the palace giving orders. You know how he likes to be obeyed.

"OFF WITH HER HEAD!" drifts in from off stage left.

Jiang: (nods his head) See what I mean?

Chou: Hurry up, Deng. Let us take a look at those ships.

Deng: All right. All right. Here goes. (begins to "swallow" the sea)

Sea holder: ("hands the sea" to Deng and slips behind the "water" and takes the ships from the other sea holder and moves them closer to Deng on the top of the water.

Ships: (come closer to Deng, almost close enough for the brothers to touch them)

Deng: (begins to "sneeze")

Jiang: (looking at Deng and pointing) Watch out! I think Deng is going to sneeze.

Yan: Quick, Li, Put your finger under his nose. (Li puts his finger under Deng's nose)

Deng: (shaking all over, but seems to gain control)

Li: (takes his finger away) Wow, that was close!!

Deng: (sneezes violently)

Ships: (are dropped to the ground)

Water: (billows up then falls to the ground as water bearer slides behind the wall)

Children: (Stunned, they point and gape at the destruction.) Oh No! Oh No!

Deng: (becomes distraught, pulls his hair and stamps his feet)

Deng: Oh, we're in so much trouble! What are we going to do?!

Li: What are WE going to do? You're the one who swallowed the sea!

Deng: You told me to. You told me to.

Chou: Oh no, here come the emperor's guards.

Guards: (rush up from stairs toward the "sea"– ready to battle the "enemy")

Peng: Where are they?

Bo: What enemy has destroyed our royal navy?

Wong: (noticing the children) Who are you?

Guards: (turn and face children at center stage – amazed and annoyed)

Deng: (bowing apologetically) I didn't mean to do it. (bows again and again) We only wanted to look more closely at the emperor's beautiful ships.

Jiang: Deng can't help it that he sneezed.

Min: What ARE you talking about? None of this makes any sense.

Peng: Hold on a minute!! You are not handsome or tall or strong or fast or graceful or smart. How could you have done anything of importance?

Li: Can it be important, even if it's bad?

Chou: Sirs, our brother Deng has a rather unusual ability. He can swallow the sea.

All Guards: (staring without believing) What?

Yan: (nodding) Yes, it is true. He can swallow the sea.

Jiang: That's what he was doing when he sneezed and accidentally destroyed the entire royal navy.

Bo: The emperor is not going to believe this.

Wong: And he's not going to like it either.

Min: Come along with us. We'd better get this over with.

Guards: (grab Deng roughly and drag him noisily downstage center and off)

Children: We're right behind you, Deng!! (follow a step or two, but then sneak back to their position at the wall and sit)

Guards and Deng: (go down the steps stage right and then back stage behind the screen)

Scene III.

Lights come to the Emperor's throne room (stage right)

Sha & Huang: (bring throne to mark and stand at attention)

Court Persons: (come up from stairs and mill around discussing the situation in whispers. Wondering what will happen. Frightened!! As Emp. Enters, bow and cower)

Emperor: (enters from the screen pacing back and forth in front of the throne)

Emperor: (shouting, very angry) My royal fleet is destroyed! My royal fleet is destroyed! My royal fleet! But how can this be? Where is the enemy? Who is responsible for this outrage!! He will be punished. (shaking fists)

Guards: (noisily approach from behind the screen with Deng)

Sha: (points toward the Guards and Deng) Here come the guards, your majesty.

Huang: (points toward the Guards and Deng) They have captured someone, but he doesn't look very important.

Peng & Bo: (dragging Deng roughly to center stage – facing the emperor)

All Imperial Guards: (come from screen and stand with guard group)

Emperor: Yes? (glaring threateningly at the guards) What's the meaning of this outrage? Why aren't you out trying to solve this crime?

Peng: (proudly facing the emperor) But we have solved it, your majesty.

Bo: (indicating Deng) This man alone has destroyed your fleet.

Emperor: <u>Preposterous</u>!!

Deng: (bowing) I'm so sorry, your majesty. My brothers and I, (pausing, looking for the right words) we just wanted to see your beautiful ships more closely, (haltingly, apologetically) so I swallowed the sea, but then I had to sneeze . . .

Emperor: Enough! (hands on hips) Are you trying to tell me that this, ah, "person" smashed my royal fleet all by himself? Well, are you?

Wong: (nodding) It seems so your majesty.

Min: He says he did it, and we don't see any enemy ships in the harbor.

Emperor: Well then, off with his head! (Clap! Clap!)

Deng: (pleading and bowing) But your majesty, I'm very sorry.

Emperor: Sorry?! Sorry?! I said, "Off with his head," IMMEDIATELY!

Guards: (backing away from the emperor, bowing and dragging Deng with them. They turn and go to upstage right and exit through screen. Then re-enter from the stairs and drag Deng to the dungeon and throw Deng in, all sit)

Children: (are outside the wall, just out of sight of the guards)

Emperor: (speaking to the rest of the court) I need a nap. Maybe this will turn out to be just a bad dream. (exits behind the screen)

Sha & Huang: (move throne against the wall and exit behind screen with Emperor)

Court Attendants: (move downstage to the stairs and sit)

Scene IV.

Lights come to stage left at the wall.

Children: (sitting in front of wall –worried and whispering)

Guards: (sitting on the bench outside the dungeon – "asleep")

Li: (standing and moving to center stage, very excited) So, what are we going to do?

Jiang: (standing and going to join Li, very excited) The Emperor, who is to be obeyed, just said that Deng should lose his head!

Chou: (runs to join them, upset) Mother and Father are going to be very angry.

Yan: (rushes to center stage) What? How can you worry about getting in trouble with our parents? Deng is about to become history.

Chou: Too bad they didn't take me. (holds his neck) They'd never be able to chop off my head.

Li: Why in the world not? Oh, that's right. You have a very strong neck.

Chou: (jumping up and down) Come with me. I'm going to see what I can do to help Deng.

Children: (move to the wall.)

Chou: (moves "through" the wall while the others watch for the guards)

Deng: (comes out to join the others)

Wong & Min: (get up and go into the dungeon, they drag out Chou downstage to the right and off, struggling and mumbling)

Yan: Do you think it will work?

Jiang: I hope so. Nothing more we can do now, but wait.

Off Stage: Whack – Whack – Whack – Whack

Wong & Min: (bring Chou upstage center, struggling and mumbling)

Sung: (to each other) How can this be happening? The Emperor says off with his head! But his head won't come off.

Ming: The Emperor always must be obeyed. He will be having our heads instead.

Guards: (push Chou into the dungeon space dejectedly)

Peng: (stops pacing, throws up his hands) It probably doesn't matter how we get rid of this unfortunate citizen as long as we get rid of him. Let's think.

Guards: (huddle for seven seconds)

Sung: (excited! Jumping up and down) I know. Let's bury him in a pit. I'll get the shovels!! (exits downstage center and down the steps to get the shovels)

Peng: (excited also) Excellent idea!

Guards: (sit down to wait outside the wall/dungeon – they sleep)

Children: (standing and moving to center stage)

Jiang: Too bad he isn't trying to bury me.

Li: Why is that?

Jiang: Don't you remember? (holds his neck) I have a very long neck.

Yan, Li, Chou, Deng: Oh, yes. (nodding to each other)

Jiang: I'll see what I can do.

Children: (move back to their wall.)

Jiang: (moves "through" the wall while the others watch for the guards)

Chou: (comes out to join the others) Wow! These guards are serious! They really tried to whack off my head!!

Sung: (comes back with a shovel.)

Peng & Sung: (reach into dungeon and drag out Jiang)

Sung: (roughly take Jiang with them down stage and down the steps) Come with us!

Chou: Do you think we can fool them again?

Yan: If we don't, our fate is sealed.

Bo & Ming: (stay outside the dungeon)

Off stage - Peng: Dig that hole deeper!!

Off stage - Sung: I'm digging as hard as I can

Peng, Sung, Ming: (rush in, dragging Jiang back up steps to center stage)

All guards jump up in surprise and amazed with fear!

Min: You're not going to believe this.

Wong: Don't tell us. Your plan didn't work. He's still alive.

Sung: We buried him as deep as we could, but his head was always above the ground. You can see he is very much still alive.

Guards: (throw Jiang back in the dungeon)

Bo: The Emperor who is not very understanding will not understand why you have not followed his orders.

Ming: I'm not going to be the one to tell him.

Peng: Wait a minute. You haven't tried everything yet. Let's think.

Guards: (huddle)

Bo: Maybe you could burn him.

Peng: Excellent idea, I'll go for some burning coals. (runs downstage and off steps)

All guards sit and wait - loitering

Yan: Too bad he isn't trying to burn you, brother. You've been unburnable from the first day I knew you.

Li: A talent no one saw much use for until this very day. I'll see what I can do.

Li: (moves "through" the wall while the others watch for the guards)

Jiang: (comes out to join the others) They never noticed anything different!

Peng: (runs back to center stage with "coals")

Guards: (reach into dungeon and drag out Li)

Wong & Min: Come with us! (roughly take Li with them down stage and down the steps)

Deng: This is starting to be fun.

Jiang: As long as the guards don't get suspicious.

Yan: I hope we can do this for as long as they can come up with crazy ideas.

Off Stage - Wong: Get more wood!

Off Stage - Min: Hurry up! (pause) This isn't working!

Guards: (rush up from the steps, push Li into the dungeon)

Bo: (watching in disbelief!!) No, no. It can't be true.

Sung: We might as well try to leave the country right now.

Ming: I don't think we should take time to go to our homes. We must leave immediately.

Min: How can we go anywhere? The boats are all destroyed. The mountains surround us.

Bo: You're right. The emperor would find us before we had a chance to hide.

Wong: Oh woe, oh woe. We are ruined.

Peng: Wait a minute. We haven't tried everything. Let's think.

Guards: (huddle together outside the dungeon)

Min: I have an idea. Just because we can't chop of his head, or bury him, or burn him, doesn't mean we can't drown him.

Peng: Excellent idea. We'll lock him in a trunk and throw him into the deepest part of the sea. I'll go get a lock for the trunk! (runs down the steps to off stage right)

Wong: (Calls after him) Hurry. The Emperor will be expecting a report.

Guards: (sit down while they wait)

Yan: Now it's my chance to be important. You DO remember that I can hold my breath forever if I have to.

Jiang: Excellent idea.

Yan: (switches with Li)

Chou: I hope those guards run out of ideas soon because we're running out of specialness.

Deng: Perhaps something will happen to distract them.

Peng: (runs back up to center stage with a lock) I have it!!

Peng & Ming: (reach in the dungeon and roughly take Yan with them down stage and down the steps)

Ad Lib mumbling about the lock and trunk

Ming & Peng: (rush on stage, dragging Yan and push him into the dungeon ahead of him. He motions to the others to follow him in.)

Guards all go in the dungeon door (mumbling) and come out the hidden opening.

Guards stumble over the children

Children hear the commotion and stumble aside to get out of the way.

Wong: Just as I suspected! Here they are! (motioning to the children huddled near the wall)

Sung: Maybe we can hide you all somewhere and the Emperor will never find out that we didn't follow his orders.

Ming: Hurry, come with us.

All Children and Guards: (run down the steps to downstage right)

Scene V.

Court Attendants & Court Guards: (move up from the steps to their places and position the throne)

Emperor: (bustles in from the hedge and moves to the throne)

Emperor: Where's my breakfast? Did anyone write the poem for the day? I cannot find my slippers.

Court Attendants: (scurry, maybe even bump into each other in their haste to obey mumbling all the while in fear)

Court Guards: (rush in saluting / bowing -move to center stage facing emperor)

Sha: O Emperor, your majesticness, a terrible thing has happened!

Huang: Our enemies must have learned of the destruction of the royal navy, your excellency.

Emperor: What? What?

Sha: Yes, your importantness, several warships are approaching our harbor as we speak.

Huang: We think they will be here within the hour, O Emperor.

Sha: What would you like us to do?

Emperor: Do? Do? I would like you to turn back time so that my royal fleet would still be in existence.

Huang: I'm afraid we can't do that.

Emperor: No, no, of course not. We must think. Call for all my guards. (clap, clap)

Guards: (rush in from the screen, looking very uncomfortable and frightened)

Emperor: We need an idea to restore our fleet and turn back the enemy!

Emperor, Guards and Court Attendants: (pacing in a circle around center stage – following the Emperor)

Emperor Stops and those following "bump" into each other – domino style

Emperor: I have it!

All Guards and CP: (stop and stare at the emperor – separate so no one has his back to the audience and the emperor is seen)

Emperor: Bring me that careless citizen who destroyed my fleet in the first place. He can just swallow the sea again and obliterate our enemies. Yes! Yes! Excellent idea!

Peng: (bowing) But, Emperor. Don't you remember? You ordered us to chop off his head.

Bo: And you always expect to be obeyed, oh imperial one.

Emperor: Quite right. Quite right. (pause) No, quite wrong. Why couldn't you have predicted that this man would turn out to be important?

Peng: Well, your highness, he wasn't handsome, or tall, or graceful, or fast, or strong. How were we to know?

Emperor: I know he wasn't all those things, but he could swallow the sea! That is turning out to be very important! If only I could turn back time before I gave that order.

Guards: (cowering and wondering what to do)

Min: (aside to the audience) Should we tell the emperor the man is still alive?

Ming: (aside to the audience) Then he would know the orders hadn't been obeyed.

Wong: (aside to the audience) But perhaps he would be happy to find out that the kingdom can be saved after all.

Min: (motions to the children back stage to come in)

Guards: (back up upstage to allow for the children entering the stage)

Deng: (comes with brothers to the throne, bowing respectfully to the emperor)

Children: (follow Deng in and bow behind him)

Deng: There's no need to turn back time, your majesty. Your guards tried their very best to obey your orders, but with the help of my family my life has been spared. (motions for Children to come forward)

Chou: (moves to center stage) You see, oh wise and patient one, we were each born with a very unusual ability.

Jiang: (moves to center stage) Yes, Chou has an iron neck. And I can stretch and stretch. And Li can't be burned. And Yan can hold his breath forever if need be.

Li: (moves to center stage) All our lives these abilities have been of little use, but this day they became very important.

Yan: (moves to center stage) Yes, we were able to save our brother's life and now he can save the kingdom. Go for it, Deng.

Emperor: (totally bewildered) I don't understand any of this, but somehow I was not obeyed and it has turned out to be a good thing. (shakes his head) Quickly, young man. (clap clap) To the harbor. Our enemies will be arriving very soon.

Deng, Children, Guards: (rush off stage behind screen and re-enter up stage from the steps to the sea)

Emperor: (waits - looking "out the window" toward the sea)

Court Attendants: (trying to see) (mumbling) Wow! Will you look at that!

"Water and ships" hand off to Deng

Emperor: Yippee! It's working!! (Suddenly, he jumps up and down and begins a wild dance)

Court Attendants: Yeah! They are saving the Empire!! (Wild cheering)

Deng: (swallows the sea)

Boats: (get closer to Deng)

Guards: Ahah! We got you now!! (seize the boats and dash them to the ground)

Water: (drops to the floor and the Water bearers move back)

Children, Guards: (run downstage center off the steps and return from the screen to center stage, showing elation)

Emperor: (joins in the celebration and then remembers his dignity)

Emperor: (on throne) Thank you, young man. Your name will be remembered by our royal storytellers for all time. How can I reward you? And your family?

Deng: Well, oh Emperor. We are very poor. Our family could use a bigger home.

Emperor: A home? Done! (clap, clap)

Chin: (hands Deng a scroll)

Chou: And a larger property to farm.

Emperor: More land? Done! (clap, clap)

Lu: (hands Chou a scroll)

Li: And more money.

Emperor: Gold and wealth? Done! (clap, clap)

Han: (hands Li a scroll)

Jiang: And we would like to be able to go to school and perhaps train for the imperial guards.

Emperor: Education and position? Done! (clap, clap)

Chin: (hands Jiang a scroll)

Yan: And oh generous and spontaneous emperor, would you mind telling our parents that we have done something important?

Emperor: You would like to be recognized as important? Of course, my son. Maybe we have all learned a few things about what is important. Send for the parents immediately. (clap, clap)

Ming & Zian: (rush behind the screen down and up steps over to the wall)

Parents are sitting near the wall at their home.

Min: (to the parents) Come with us quickly! The Emperor requests your presence!

Ming: Your children have done something important!

Zian: I told you they were fine children!

Mah: I'll believe it when I see it.

Parents and Min & Zian exit downstage right and come back up to behind the screen.

Chin: (excited but then sad and afraid) Oh, Emperor, who insists on being obeyed. I wrote the royal poem for the day, but the short, weak scribe who was copying it spilled the ink in a very clumsy way and smeared the paper beyond repair. The poem is lost.

Emperor: What? What? No Poem? Well then, Off with . . . ah . . .(pause hands ready to clap the order)

ALL: (turn and stare at the emperor, amazed!)

Emperor: (catches himself in a habit) Oh, well. Ha, ha. Even an emperor can make a mistake once in a while. It's important to have a second chance. I order everyone to take a holiday to celebrate our victory – and (looking at them all severely) - and I expect to be obeyed! (laughs)

Chin &Han: Ha Ha, (timidly they laugh a little, then smile and nod)

Min & Zian: (return with parents from screen)

Parents: Bow to the Emperor and embrace children.

All continue to celebrate. -   Curtain !!

Aesop's Fables

THE FOX AND THE GRAPES

A hungry Fox saw some fine bunches of Grapes hanging from a vine that was trained along a high trellis, and did his best to reach them by jumping as high as he could into the air. But it was all in vain, for they were just out of reach: so he gave up trying, and walked away with an air of dignity and unconcern, remarking, "I thought those Grapes were ripe, but I see now they are quite sour."

THE GOOSE THAT LAID THE GOLDEN EGGS

A Man and his Wife had the good fortune to possess a Goose which laid a Golden Egg every day. Lucky though they were, they soon began to think they were not getting rich fast enough, and, imagining the bird must be made of gold inside, they decided to kill it in order to secure the whole store of precious metal at once. But when they cut it open they found it was just like any other goose. Thus, they neither got rich all at once, as they had hoped, nor enjoyed any longer the daily addition to their wealth.

Much wants more and loses all.

THE CAT AND THE MICE

There was once a house that was overrun with Mice. A Cat heard of this, and said to herself, "That's the place for me," and off she went and took up her quarters in the house, and caught the Mice one by one and ate them. At last the Mice could stand it no longer, and they determined to take to their holes and stay there. "That's awkward," said the Cat to herself: "the only thing to do is to <u>coax</u> them out by a trick." So she considered a while, and then climbed up the wall and let herself hang down by her hind legs from a peg, and pretended to be dead. By and by a Mouse peeped out and saw the Cat hanging there. "Aha!" it cried, "you're very clever, madam, no doubt: but you may turn yourself into a bag of meal hanging there, if you like, yet you won't catch us coming anywhere near you."

If you are wise you won't be <u>deceive</u>d by the innocent airs of those whom you have once found to be dangerous.

THE MISCHIEVOUS DOG

There was once a Dog who used to snap at people and bite them without any <u>provocation,</u> and who was a great nuisance to everyone who came to his master's house. So his master fastened a bell round his neck to warn people of his presence. The Dog was very proud of the bell, and strutted about tinkling it with immense satisfaction. But an old dog came up to him and said, "The fewer airs you give yourself the better, my friend. You don't think, do you, that your bell was given you as a reward of merit? On the contrary, it is a badge of disgrace."

Notoriety is often mistaken for fame.

THE CHARCOAL-BURNER AND THE FULLER

There was once a Charcoal-burner who lived and worked by himself. A Fuller, however, happened to come and settle in the same neighborhood; and the Charcoal-burner, having made his acquaintance and finding he was an agreeable sort of fellow, asked him if he would come and share his house: "We shall get to know one another better that way," he said, "and, beside, our household expenses will be <u>diminishe</u>d." The Fuller thanked him, but replied, "I couldn't think of it, sir: why, everything I

66

take such pains to whiten would be blackened in no time by your charcoal."

THE MICE IN COUNCIL

Once upon a time all the Mice met together in Council, and discussed the best means of securing themselves against the attacks of the cat. After several suggestions had been debated, a Mouse of some standing and experience got up and said, "I think I have hit upon a plan which will ensure our safety in the future, provided you approve and carry it out. It is that we should fasten a bell round the neck of our enemy the cat, which will by its tinkling warn us of her approach." This proposal was warmly applauded, and it had been already decided to adopt it, when an old Mouse got upon his feet and said, "I agree with you all that the plan before us is an admirable one: but may I ask who is going to bell the cat?"

THE BAT AND THE WEASELS

A Bat fell to the ground and was caught by a Weasel, and was just going to be killed and eaten when it begged to be let go. The Weasel said he couldn't do that because he was an enemy of all birds on principle. "Oh, but," said the Bat, "I'm not a bird at all: I'm a mouse." "So you are," said the Weasel, "now I come to look at you"; and he let it go. Some time after this the Bat was caught in just the same way by another Weasel, and, as before, begged for its life. "No," said the Weasel, "I never let a mouse go by any chance." "But I'm not a mouse," said the Bat; "I'm a bird." "Why, so you are," said the Weasel; and he too let the Bat go.

Look and see which way the wind blows before you commit yourself.

THE DOG AND THE SOW

[Note: A sow is mother pig.]

A Dog and a Sow were arguing and each claimed that its own young ones were finer than those of any other animal. "Well," said the Sow at last, "mine can see, at any rate, when they come into the world: but yours are born blind."

THE FOX AND THE CROW

A Crow was sitting on a branch of a tree with a piece of cheese in her beak when a Fox observed her and set his wits to work to discover some way of getting the cheese. Coming and standing under the tree he looked up and said, "What a noble bird I see above me! Her beauty is without equal, the <u>hue</u> of her plumage <u>exquisite</u>. If only her voice is as sweet as her looks are fair, she ought without doubt to be Queen of the Birds." The Crow was hugely flattered by this, and just to show the Fox that she could sing she gave a loud caw. Down came the cheese, of course, and the Fox, snatching it up, said, "You have a voice, madam, I see: what you want is wits."

THE HORSE AND THE GROOM

There was once a Groom who used to spend long hours clipping and combing the Horse of which he had charge, but who daily stole a portion of his allowance of oats, and sold it for his own profit. The Horse gradually got into worse and worse condition, and at last cried to the Groom, "If you really want me to look sleek and well, you must comb me less and feed me more."

THE WOLF AND THE LAMB

A Wolf came upon a Lamb straying from the flock, and felt some compunction about taking the life of so helpless a creature without some plausible excuse; so he cast about for a grievance and said at last, "Last year, sirrah, you grossly insulted me." "That is impossible, sir," bleated the Lamb, "for I wasn't born then." "Well," retorted the Wolf, "you feed in my pastures." "That cannot be," replied the Lamb, "for I have never yet tasted grass." "You drink from my spring, then," continued the Wolf. "Indeed, sir," said the poor Lamb, "I have never yet drunk anything but my mother's milk." "Well, anyhow," said the Wolf, "I'm not going without my dinner": and he sprang upon the Lamb and devoured it without more ado.

THE PEACOCK AND THE CRANE

A Peacock taunted a Crane with the dullness of her plumage. "Look at my brilliant colors," said she, "and see how much finer they are than your poor feathers." "I am not denying," replied the Crane, that yours are far gayer than mine; but when it comes to flying I can soar into the clouds, whereas you are confined to the earth like any dunghill cock."

THE CAT AND THE BIRDS

A Cat heard that the Birds in an aviary were ailing. So he got himself up as a doctor, and, taking with him a set of the instruments proper to his profession, presented himself at the door, and inquired after the health of the Birds. "We shall do very well," they replied, without letting him in, "when we've seen the last of you."

A villain may disguise himself, but he will not <u>deceive</u> the wise.

THE SPENDTHRIFT AND THE SWALLOW

A Spendthrift, who had wasted his fortune, and had nothing left but the clothes in which he stood, saw a Swallow one fine day in early spring. Thinking that summer had come, and that he could now do without his coat, he went and sold it for what it would fetch. A change, however, took place in the weather, and there came a sharp frost which killed the unfortunate Swallow. When the spendthrift saw its dead body he cried, "Miserable bird! Thanks to you I am perishing of cold myself."

One swallow does not make summer.

THE OLD WOMAN AND THE DOCTOR

An Old Woman became almost totally blind from a disease of the eyes, and, after consulting a Doctor, made an agreement with him in the presence of witnesses that she should pay him a high fee if he cured her, while if he failed he was to receive nothing. The Doctor accordingly prescribed a course of treatment, and every time he paid her a visit he took away with him some article out of the house, until at last, when he visited her for the last time, and the cure was complete, there was nothing left. When the Old Woman saw that the house was empty she refused to pay him his fee; and, after repeated refusals on her part, he sued her before the magistrates for payment of her debt. On being brought into court she was ready with her defense. "The claimant," said she, "has stated the facts about our agreement correctly. I undertook to pay him a fee if he cured me, and he, on his part, promised to charge nothing if he failed. Now, he says I am cured; but I say that I am blinder than ever, and I can prove what I say. When my eyes were bad I could at any rate see well enough to be aware that my house contained a certain amount of furniture and other things; but now, when according to him I am cured, I am entirely unable to see anything there at all."

THE MOON AND HER MOTHER

The Moon once begged her Mother to make her a gown. "How can I?" replied she; "there's no fitting your figure. At one time you're a New Moon, and at another you're a Full Moon; and between whiles you're neither one nor the other."

THE LION AND THE MOUSE

A Lion asleep in his lair was waked up by a Mouse running over his face. Losing his temper he seized it with his paw and was about to kill it. The Mouse, terrified, piteously entreated him to spare its life. "Please let me go," it cried, "and one day I will repay you for your kindness." The idea of so insignificant a creature ever being able to do anything for him amused the Lion so much that he laughed aloud, and good-humoredly let it go. But the Mouse's chance came, after all. One day the Lion got entangled in a net which had been spread for game by some hunters, and the Mouse heard and recognized his roars of anger and ran to the spot. Without more ado it set to work to gnaw the ropes with its teeth, and succeeded before long in setting the Lion free. "There!" said the Mouse, "you laughed at me when I promised I would repay you: but now you see, even a Mouse can help a Lion."

THE CROW AND THE PITCHER

A thirsty Crow found a Pitcher with some water in it, but so little was there that, try as she might, she could not reach it with her beak, and it seemed as though she would die of thirst within sight of the remedy. At last she hit upon a clever plan. She began dropping pebbles into the Pitcher, and with each pebble the water rose a little higher until at last it reached the brim, and the knowing bird was enabled to quench her thirst.

Necessity is the mother of invention.

THE BOYS AND THE FROGS

Some mischievous Boys were playing on the edge of a pond, and, catching sight of some Frogs swimming about in the shallow water, they began to amuse themselves by pelting them with stones, and they killed several of them. At last one of the Frogs put his head out of the water and said, "Oh, stop! stop! I beg of you: what is sport to you is death to us."

THE NORTH WIND AND THE SUN

A dispute arose between the North Wind and the Sun, each claiming that he was stronger than the other. At last they agreed to try their powers upon a traveller, to see which could soonest strip him of his cloak. The North Wind had the first try; and, gathering up all his force for the attack, he came whirling furiously down upon the man, and caught up his cloak as though he would wrest it from him by one single effort: but the harder he blew, the more closely the man wrapped it round himself. Then came the turn of the Sun. At first he beamed gently upon the traveller, who soon unclasped his cloak and walked on with it hanging loosely about his shoulders: then he shone forth in his full strength, and the man, before he had gone many steps, was glad to throw his cloak right off and complete his journey more lightly clad.

Persuasion is better than force

THE MISTRESS AND HER SERVANTS

A Widow, thrifty and industrious, had two servants, whom she kept pretty hard at work. They were not allowed to lie long abed in the mornings, but the old lady had them up and doing as soon as the cock crew. They disliked intensely having to get up at such an hour, especially in winter-time: and they thought that if it were not for the cock waking up their Mistress so horribly early, they could sleep longer. So they caught it and wrung its neck. But they weren't prepared for the consequences. For what happened was that their Mistress, not hearing the cock crow as usual, waked them up earlier than ever, and set them to work in the middle of the night.

THE HARES AND THE FROGS

The Hares once gathered together and lamented the unhappiness of their lot, exposed as they were to dangers on all sides and lacking the strength and the courage to hold their own. Men, dogs, birds and beasts of prey were all their enemies, and killed and devoured them daily: and sooner than endure such persecution any longer, they one and all determined to end their miserable lives. Thus resolved and desperate, they rushed in a body towards a neighboring pool, intending to drown themselves. On the bank were sitting a number of Frogs, who, when they heard the noise of the Hares as they ran, with one accord leaped into the water and hid themselves in the depths. Then one of the older Hares who was wiser than the rest cried out to his companions, "Stop, my friends, take heart; don't let us destroy ourselves after all: see, here are creatures who are afraid of us, and who must, therefore, be still more timid than ourselves."

THE FOX AND THE STORK

A Fox invited a Stork to dinner, at which the only fare provided was a large flat dish of soup. The Fox lapped it up with great relish, but the Stork with her long bill tried in vain to partake of the savoury broth. Her evident distress caused the sly Fox much amusement. But not long after the Stork invited him in turn, and set before him a pitcher with a long and narrow neck, into which she could get her bill with ease. Thus, while she enjoyed her

73

dinner, the Fox sat by hungry and helpless, for it was impossible for him to reach the tempting contents of the vessel.

THE WOLF IN SHEEP'S CLOTHING

A Wolf resolved to disguise himself in order that he might prey upon a flock of sheep without fear of detection. So he clothed himself in a sheepskin, and slipped among the sheep when they were out at pasture. He completely <u>deceive</u>d the shepherd, and when the flock was penned for the night he was shut in with the rest. But that very night as it happened, the shepherd, requiring a supply of mutton for the table, laid hands on the Wolf in mistake for a Sheep, and killed him with his knife on the spot.

THE STAG IN THE OX-STALL
[Note: A stag is a male deer.]

A Stag, chased from his lair by the hounds, took refuge in a farmyard, and, entering a stable where a number of oxen were stalled, thrust himself under a pile of hay in a vacant stall, where he lay concealed, all but the tips of his horns. Presently one of the Oxen said to him, "What has induced you to come in here? Aren't you aware of the risk you are running of being captured by the herdsmen?" To which he replied, "Pray let me stay for the present. When night comes I shall easily escape under cover of the dark." In the course of the afternoon more than one of the farm-hands came in, to attend to the wants of the cattle, but not one of them noticed the presence of the Stag, who accordingly began to congratulate himself on his escape and to express his gratitude to the Oxen. "We wish you well," said the one who had spoken before, "but you are not out of danger yet. If the master comes, you will certainly be found out, for nothing ever escapes his <u>keen</u> eyes." Presently, sure enough, in he came, and made a great to-do about the way the Oxen were kept. "The beasts are starving," he cried; "here, give them more hay, and

74

put plenty of litter under them." As he spoke, he seized an armful himself from the pile where the Stag lay concealed, and at once detected him. Calling his men, he had him seized at once and killed for the table.

THE MILKMAID AND HER PAIL

A farmer's daughter had been out to milk the cows, and was returning to the dairy carrying her pail of milk upon her head. As she walked along, she started thinking: "The milk in this pail will provide me with cream, which I will make into butter and take to market to sell. With the money I will buy a number of eggs, and these, when hatched, will produce chickens, and by and by I shall have quite a large poultry-yard. Then I shall sell some of my fowls, and with the money which they will bring in I will buy myself a new gown, which I shall wear when I go to the fair; and all the young fellows will admire it, but I shall toss my head and have nothing to say to them." Forgetting all about the pail, and suiting the action to the word, she tossed her head. Down went the pail, all the milk was spilled, and all her fine castles in the air vanished in a moment!

Do not count your chickens before they are hatched.

THE FOX AND THE MONKEY

A Fox and a Monkey were on the road together, and fell into a dispute as to which of the two was the better born. They kept it up for some time, till they came to a place where the road passed through a cemetery full of monuments, when the Monkey stopped and looked about him and gave a great sigh. "Why do you sigh?" said the Fox. The Monkey pointed to the tombs and replied, "All the monuments that you see here were put up in honor of my forefathers, who in their day were eminent men." The Fox was speechless for a moment, but quickly recovering he said, "Oh! don't stop at any lie, sir; you're quite safe: I'm sure none of your ancestors will rise up and expose you."

Boasters brag most when they cannot be detected.

THE FIR-TREE AND THE BRAMBLE

A Fir-tree was boasting to a Bramble, and said, somewhat contemptuously, "You poor creature, you are of no use whatever. Now, look at me: I am useful for all sorts of things, particularly when men build houses; they can't do without me then." But the Bramble replied, "Ah, that's all very well: but you wait till they come with axes and saws to cut you down, and then you'll wish you were a Bramble and not a Fir."

Better poverty without a care than wealth with its many obligations.

THE DOG, THE COCK, AND THE FOX

A Dog and a Cock became great friends, and agreed to travel together. At nightfall the Cock flew up into the branches of a tree to roost, while the Dog curled himself up inside the trunk, which was hollow. At break of day the Cock woke up and crew, as usual. A Fox heard, and, wishing to make a breakfast of him, came and stood under the tree and begged him to come down. "I should so like," said he, "to make the acquaintance of one who has such a beautiful voice." The Cock replied, "Would you just wake my porter who sleeps at the foot of the tree? He'll open the door and let you in." The Fox accordingly rapped on the trunk, when out rushed the Dog and tore him in pieces.

THE GNAT AND THE BULL

A Gnat alighted on one of the horns of a Bull, and remained sitting there for a considerable time. When it had rested sufficiently and was about to fly away, it said to the Bull, "Do you mind if I go now?" The Bull merely raised his eyes and remarked, without interest, "It's all one to me; I didn't notice when you came, and I shan't know when you go away."

We may often be of more consequence in our own eyes than in the eyes of our neighbors.

THE BEAR AND THE TRAVELERS

Two Travelers were on the road together, when a Bear suddenly appeared on the scene. Before he observed them, one made for a tree at the side of the road, and climbed up into the branches and hid there. The other was not so nimble as his companion; and, as he could not escape, he threw himself on the ground and pretended to be dead. The Bear came up and sniffed all round him, but he kept perfectly still and held his breath: for they say that a bear will not touch a dead body. The Bear took him for a corpse, and went away. When the coast was clear, the Traveler in the tree came down, and asked the other what it was the Bear had whispered to him when he put his mouth to his ear. The other replied, "He told me never again to travel with a friend who deserts you at the first sign of danger."

Misfortune tests the sincerity of friendship.

THE SLAVE AND THE LION

A Slave ran away from his master, by whom he had been most cruelly treated, and, in order to avoid capture, betook himself into the desert. As he wandered about in search of food and shelter, he came to a cave, which he entered and found to be unoccupied. Really, however, it was a Lion's den, and almost immediately, to the horror of the wretched fugitive, the Lion himself appeared. The man gave himself up for lost: but, to his utter astonishment, the Lion, instead of springing upon him and devouring him, came and fawned upon him, at the same time whining and lifting up his paw. Observing it to be much swollen and inflamed, he examined it and found a large thorn embedded in the ball of the foot. He accordingly removed it and dressed the wound as well as he could: and in course of time it healed up completely. The Lion's gratitude was unbounded; he looked upon the man as his friend, and they shared the cave for some time together. A day came, however, when the Slave began to long for the society of his fellow-men, and he bade farewell to the Lion and returned to the town. Here he was presently recognized and carried off in chains to his former master, who resolved to make an example of him, and ordered that he should be thrown to the beasts at the next public spectacle in the theatre. On the fatal day the beasts were loosed into the arena, and among the rest a Lion of huge bulk and ferocious aspect; and then the wretched Slave was cast in among them. What was the amazement of the spectators, when the Lion after one glance bounded up to him and lay down at his feet with every expression of affection and delight! It was his old friend of the cave! The audience clamored that the Slave's life should be spared: and the governor of the town, marveling at such gratitude and fidelity in a beast, decreed that both should receive their liberty.

THE FLEA AND THE MAN

A Flea bit a Man, and bit him again, and again, till he could stand it no longer, but made a thorough search for it, and at last succeeded in catching it. Holding it between his finger and thumb, he said—or rather shouted, so angry was he--"Who are you, pray, you wretched little creature, that you make so free with my person?" The Flea, terrified, whimpered in a weak little voice, "Oh, sir! pray let me go; don't kill me! I am such a little thing that I can't do you much harm." But the Man laughed and said, "I am going to kill you now, at once: whatever is bad has got to be destroyed, no matter how slight the harm it does."

Do not waste your pity on a scamp.

THE BOY AND THE SNAILS

A Farmer's Boy went looking for Snails, and, when he had picked up both his hands full, he set about making a fire at which to roast them; for he meant to eat them. When it got well alight and the Snails began to feel the heat, they gradually withdrew more and more into their shells with the hissing noise they always make when they do so. When the Boy heard it, he said, "You abandoned creatures, how can you find heart to whistle when your houses are burning?"

THE APES AND THE TWO TRAVELERS

Two men were travelling together, one of whom never spoke the truth, whereas the other never told a lie: and they came in the course of their travels to the land of Apes. The King of the Apes, hearing of their arrival, ordered them to be brought before him; and by way of impressing them with his magnificence, he received them sitting on a throne, while the Apes, his subjects, were ranged in long rows on either side of him. When the Travelers came into his presence he asked them what they thought of him as a King. The lying Traveler said, "Sire, everyone must see that you are a most noble and mighty monarch." "And what do you think of my subjects?" continued the King. "They," said the Traveler, "are in every way worthy of their royal master." The Ape was so delighted with his answer that he gave him a very handsome present. The other Traveler thought that if his companion was rewarded so splendidly for telling a lie, he himself would certainly receive a still greater reward for telling the truth; so, when the Ape turned to him and said, "And what, sir, is your opinion?" he replied, "I think you are a very fine Ape, and all your subjects are fine Apes too." The King of the Apes was so enraged at his reply that he ordered him to be taken away and clawed to death.

THE SHEPHERD'S BOY AND THE WOLF

A Shepherd's Boy was tending his flock near a village, and thought it would be great fun to <u>hoax</u> the villagers by pretending that a Wolf was attacking the sheep: so he shouted out, "Wolf! wolf!" and when the people came running up he laughed at them for their pains. He did this more than once, and every time the villagers found they had been <u>hoax</u>ed, for there was no Wolf at all. At last a Wolf really did come, and the Boy cried, "Wolf! wolf!" as loud as he could: but the people were so used to hearing him call that they took no notice of his cries for help. And so the Wolf had it all his own way, and killed off sheep after sheep at his leisure.

You cannot believe a liar even when he tells the truth.

THE FOX AND THE GOAT

A Fox fell into a well and was unable to get out again. By and by a thirsty Goat came by, and seeing the Fox in the well asked him if the water was good. "Good?" said the Fox, "it's the best water I ever tasted in all my life. Come down and try it yourself." The Goat thought of nothing but the prospect of quenching his thirst, and jumped in at once. When he had had enough to drink, he looked about, like the Fox, for some way of getting out, but could find none. Presently the Fox said, "I have an idea. You stand on your hind legs, and plant your forelegs firmly against the side of the well, and then I'll climb on to your back, and, from there, by stepping on your horns, I can get out. And when I'm out, I'll help you out too." The Goat did as he was requested, and the Fox climbed on to his back and so out of the well; and then he coolly walked away. The Goat called loudly after him and reminded him of his promise to help him out: but the Fox merely turned and said, "If you had as much sense in your head as you have hair in your beard you wouldn't have got into the well without making certain that you could get out again."

Look before your leap.

THE FISHERMAN AND THE SPRAT

A Fisherman cast his net into the sea, and when he drew it up again it contained nothing but a single Sprat that begged to be put back into the water. "I'm only a little fish now," it said, "but I shall grow big one day, and then if you come and catch me again I shall be of some use to you." But the Fisherman replied, "Oh, no, I shall keep you now I've got you: if I put you back, should I ever see you again? Not likely!"

THE BOASTING TRAVELER

A Man once went abroad on his travels, and when he came home he had wonderful tales to tell of the things he had done in foreign countries. Among other things, he said he had taken part in a jumping-match at Rhodes, and had done a wonderful jump which no one could beat. "Just go to Rhodes and ask them," he said; "everyone will tell you it's true." But one of those who were listening said, "If you can jump as well as all that, we needn't go to Rhodes to prove it. Let's just imagine this is Rhodes for a minute: and now--jump!"

Deeds, not words.

THE CRAB AND HIS MOTHER

An Old Crab said to her son, "Why do you walk sideways like that, my son? You ought to walk straight." The Young Crab replied, "Show me how, dear mother, and I'll follow your example." The Old Crab tried, but tried in vain, and then saw how foolish she had been to find <u>fault</u> with her child.

Example is better than precept.

THE BOY BATHING

A Boy was bathing in a river and got out of his depth, and was in great danger of being drowned. A man who was passing along a road heard his cries for help, and went to the riverside and began to scold him for being so careless as to get into deep water, but made no attempt to help him. "Oh, sir," cried the Boy, "please help me first and scold me afterwards."

Give assistance, not advice, in a crisis.

THE QUACK FROG

Once upon a time a Frog came forth from his home in the marshes and proclaimed to all the world that he was a learned physician, skilled in drugs and able to cure all diseases. Among the crowd was a Fox, who called out, "You a doctor! Why, how can you set up to heal others when you cannot even cure your own lame legs and blotched and wrinkled skin?"

Physician, heal thyself.

THE SWOLLEN FOX

A hungry Fox found in a hollow tree a quantity of bread and meat, which some shepherds had placed there against their return. Delighted with his find he slipped in through the narrow aperture and greedily devoured it all. But when he tried to get out again he found himself so swollen after his big meal that he could not squeeze through the hole, and fell to whining and groaning over his misfortune. Another Fox, happening to pass that way, came and asked him what the matter was; and, on learning the state of the case, said, "Well, my friend, I see nothing for it but for you to stay where you are till you shrink to your former size; you'll get out then easily enough."

THE MOUSE, THE FROG, AND THE HAWK

A Mouse and a Frog struck up a friendship; they were not well mated, for the Mouse lived entirely on land, while the Frog was equally at home on land or in the water. In order that they might never be separated, the Frog tied himself and the Mouse together by the leg with a piece of thread. As long as they kept on dry land all went fairly well; but, coming to the edge of a pool, the Frog jumped in, taking the Mouse with him, and began swimming about and croaking with pleasure. The unhappy Mouse, however, was soon drowned, and floated about on the surface in the wake of the Frog. There he was spied by a Hawk, who pounced down on him and seized him in his talons. The Frog was unable to loose the knot which bound him to the Mouse, and thus was carried off along with him and eaten by the Hawk.

THE BOY AND THE NETTLES

A Boy was gathering berries from a hedge when his hand was stung by a Nettle. Smarting with the pain, he ran to tell his mother, and said to her between his sobs, "I only touched it ever so lightly, mother." "That's just why you got stung, my son," she said; "if you had grasped it firmly, it wouldn't have hurt you in the least."

THE PEASANT AND THE APPLE-TREE

A Peasant had an Apple-tree growing in his garden, which bore no fruit, but merely served to provide a shelter from the heat for the sparrows and grasshoppers which sat and chirped in its branches. Disappointed at its barrenness he determined to cut it down, and went and fetched his axe for the purpose. But when the sparrows and the grasshoppers saw what he was about to do, they begged him to spare it, and said to him, "If you destroy the tree we shall have to seek shelter elsewhere, and you will no longer have our merry chirping to enliven your work in the garden." He, however, refused to listen to them, and set to work with a will to cut through the trunk. A few strokes showed that it was hollow inside and contained a swarm of bees and a large store of honey. Delighted with his find he threw down his axe, saying, "The old tree is worth keeping after all."

Utility is most men's test of worth

THE JACKDAW AND THE PIGEONS
[A jackdaw is a kind of crow.]

A Jackdaw, watching some Pigeons in a farmyard, was filled with envy when he saw how well they were fed, and determined to disguise himself as one of them, in order to secure a share of the good things they enjoyed. So he painted himself white from head to foot and joined the flock; and, so long as he was silent, they never suspected that he was not a pigeon like themselves. But one day he was unwise enough to start chattering, when they at once saw through his disguise and pecked him so unmercifully that he was glad to escape and join his own kind

84

again. But the other jackdaws did not recognize him in his white dress, and would not let him feed with them, but drove him away: and so he became a homeless wanderer for his pains.

THE DOG IN THE MANGER

A Dog was lying in a Manger on the hay which had been put there for the cattle, and when they came and tried to eat, he growled and snapped at them and wouldn't let them get at their food. "What a selfish beast," said one of them to his companions; "he can't eat himself and yet he won't let those eat who can."

THE TWO BAGS

Every man carries Two Bags about with him, one in front and one behind, and both are packed full of faults. The Bag in front contains his neighbors' faults, the one behind his own. Hence it is that men do not see their own faults, but never fail to see those of others.

If you find a mistake in any of our books, please contact us through genesiscurriculum.com to let us know, and we will get it fixed.

The Genesis Curriculum takes the Bible and turns it into lessons for your homeschool. Daily lessons include Bible reading, memory verse, spelling, handwriting, vocabulary, grammar, Biblical language, science, social studies, writing, and thinking through discussion questions.

The Genesis Curriculum uses a complete book of the Bible for one full year. The curriculum is being made using both Old and New Testament books. Find us online at genesiscurriculum.com to read about the latest developments in this expanding curriculum.

The Easy Peasy All-in-One Homeschool is a free, complete online homeschool. There are 180 days of ready-to-go assignments for every level and every subject. It's created for your children to work as independently as you want them to. Preschool through high school is available as well as courses ranging from English, math, science and history to art, music, computer, thinking, physical education and health. A daily Bible lesson is offered as well. The mission of Easy Peasy is to enable those to homeschool who otherwise thought they couldn't.

71919838R00053

Made in the USA
Columbia, SC
09 June 2017